12 Easy Steps is a trademark for books in a series so if you have an idea for *12 Easy Steps,* contact me and we will work out an agreement.

Please address inquiries to:

Connie J. Schlosberg

Director, Integrity Creative Business LLC

www.integritycreativebusiness.com

This e-book is dedicated to everyone who wants to learn how to write a resume, but needs a helping hand in a short amount of time.

ACKNOWLEDGEMENTS

I would like to thank everyone who made this e-book possible – you know who you are (at least, I think). Of course, as always, I am grateful to my family and friends for their support and assistance. Most importantly, I would like to thank my husband for believing in me and being my true love. To my daughter, you are my inspiration. Thank you for just being who you are.

I would also like to thank all the authors of all those how-to and instructional books that I read. If I hadn't studied them through and through, I may never have come up with the quick and easy, down and dirty way of learning.

I am thankful for all the hiring authorities who never responded to my resumes, cover letters, emails, etc. Why? Because I wouldn't have had so many rewrites and lessons learned on writing resumes. Nevertheless it was still mean of you not to respond to me.

Most of all, I would like to thank **YOU**. Thank you for purchasing this e-book. I am grateful to get to hold your hand through the process. Remember – who you are is not defined by your job. It is just something you do to make money to do the things you really want to do.

Table of Contents

Introduction

What will you gain from this workbook?

This workbook can help you build the resume that makes your greatest impression whether you are:

- Creating your resume to get your first professional job
- Revamping an old resume due to a job change or re-entry to the workplace
- Planning a career change where the old resume just won't do

After completing this workbook, you should be able to:

- Select the best type of format for your resume
- Put together content using words specific to your career aspirations
- Develop your resume with a professional format that employers want to see
- Prepare an effective and meaningful resume to support your goals

Step 1
Resume Types

What type are you?

Writing your resume should be more than just information regarding your education and experiences and sending it out to potential employers. Resumes written for the specific position and employer will set your resume apart from your competitors. Consider your resume a template that you will adjust for each position that you apply for.

In this step, you will:

- Learn about the different types of resumes
- Choose which type will work best for you based your work history and your career ambitions

Use one of the worksheets (chronological, functional, combination) to help you build your resume. The worksheets can downloaded at http://www.integritycreativebusiness.com/resume-worksheet-templates.html (password is: 12easysteps).

There are three different resume types

Chronological Resume: *This is the most common type of resume showing a straight career path starting with your most recent job.*

If your past jobs and experiences are all related to your next career goal, the chronological resume is the best choice. This resume is arranged to show your past positions in a linear format.

Functional Resume: *This is the type of format to use if you are looking to change your career.*

When your past jobs and experiences are not related to your next career aspirations, you will want a resume that focuses on the skills you have that match the skills and requirements of the position that you desire. While you will still need to list your work history at the end of the resume, your skills and knowledge should be the center of attraction. In this way, you will show the employer that you have the necessary skills to do the job while minimizing where you got the experience.

Combination Resume: *The most common format for recent college graduates.*

The combination resume is your best bet when some of your past jobs and experiences relate to your goals but others do not. You can organize your experiences by different categories - ones that are related to the prospective job and ones that are not.

You should carefully decide now which resume type is best for your situation. From there, you can create your draft using the worksheet and the specific resume type example (shown above) as your model.

Step 2
Job Search Research

Why do I need to do research for job searching?

You cannot create an effective resume without knowing what it is that you want to do and to be honest, with whom it is that you are trying to please. You should know what type of position that you are applying for. You also need to consider the employers and industries that hire your desired position. How can you effectively write a resume without knowing what information they are looking for and present it to them in the way that they want to read it?

Once you have an idea of what types of positions you want and think you can qualify for, you should narrow it down to about two or three similar positions. Find the job descriptions for these positions as you will be using them to help you prepare your resume for your job search.

Word of Caution - Do not fall victim to paralysis by analysis. Do your researches and make a decision or you'll never get to create your resume. This process should not take more than a few hours or a day at most.

Where can I look for job descriptions?

- *Occupational Outlook Handbook*: The Occupational Outlook Handbook is managed by the Bureau for Labor Statistics and is an A to Z reference manual for hundreds of different job types. Please visit http://www.bls.gov/oco/.
- *Wet Feet*: WetFeet was started by Stanford MBAs Gary Alpert and Steve Pollock who were looking for information for their next career moves but none existed at the time. *Voilà!* They created numerous products to help you research your next career move. Check them out at www.wetfeet.com.
- *Federal Government:* For federal government jobs, please visit www.usajobs.gov.
- *State Governments:* For state government jobs, please visit each state's website. Typically the web address is www.state.   .us. Simply replace the initials for each state in the blank between state and us. For example, www.state.co.us for Colorado's website.

- *Job Search Engines:* Job search engines will have the job descriptions for all of their open positions. Just search on the position that you are looking for. There are numerous job search engines out there but start with the big ones:
  - www.monster.com
  - www.hotjobs.com
  - www.careerbuilder.com
  - www.linkup.com
  - www.jobcentral.com
  - www.indeed.com
- *Search Engines*: You can also use www.google.com, www.bing.com or www.yahoo.com to find out more about the type of work you want.

What should I do with these job postings and research?

After researching the job descriptions that interest you, you should narrow it down to at most three. Once again, look for job descriptions from a few jobs in the same career field (e.g., editor, copyeditor, and proofreader) and from a few different employers within the industry you want to work in. This way you will have a good understanding of what is expected and how you can write your resume to fit the job types and industries that you are looking for.

Also, keep in mind that job titles differ for each organization and industry. You may want to search on job categories rather than just titles. A great place to find out what job categories you are interested in is the Occupational Outlook Handbook available at http://www.bls.gov/oco/.

Your next steps should be to:

1. Print the position description(s)
2. Read them carefully notating on the descriptions what you have already done in some capacity
3. Visit the employers' web sites
4. At their websites, review the information regarding the employer's expectation of employees, mission/vision statements, core values, etc.
5. Print the information to use as a guide when describing your experiences

So where do we go from here?

Now that you have the details on what you want to do, it's time to build your resume.

Step 3
Header

Of course, you want the prospective employer to know your name and how to get a hold of you for an interview. So naturally the best place for this information is at the top of the page. You can create a header in any word processing software program. Once you create the header, it will appear on every page of your resume document. This step gives a breakdown of what to include in the header including format along with a few examples for you to choose from. Obviously changing it to your own information!

What do I need to include in the header?

1. **Name**. Try to use your full name. You may include your nickname in quotes between your first and last name such as James "Skip" Peterson. You should use your discretion if nicknames are appropriate depending on the job you are applying for and the research you have done on the position and the companies.
2. **Home Address**.
3. **Phone No**. You may include both your cell phone and land line numbers.
4. **Email Address**. Please make sure your email address is appropriate. You really don't want your future employer to wonder why you chose hotchick@yahoo.com. You can create a free email account with such sites as msn.com and gmail.com. Setup an account using your first and last name. If you have a common name, you can play a bit with the setup such as jsmith@msn.com or work in your middle name or initial as in johndsmith@gmail.com.
5. **Website**. If you have a professional website, blog and/or portfolio site where employers may view your work, by all means include it here. Avoid including social media sites unless they are conducive to the job you are applying for. You may use a link to your professional social media site such as LinkedIn.

How should I format it?

There are many options for formatting your header. The style is your choice; however, you want to keep it in a format that anyone can read and understand. Therefore, the font and size should be traditional. You can't go wrong with Arial, Times New Roman, and Courier. Keep the size between 10 and 12. Also, highlight your name in bold to make yourself stand out!

Some examples for you to try:

JOHN D. SMITH
1313 Mockingbird Lane
Hollywood, CA 90028
(323) 111-2222
johnsmith@gmail.com
www.johnsmith.com

Mary Jones
123 Elm Drive
Allentown, PA 18103
(619) 333-0000
maj@msn.com

Jason W. Sheltfield

456 Main Street
Colorado Springs, CO 18106

610-456-8899
jwsheltfield@yahoo.com

You get the picture. Easy so far. Let's move on to the next step.

Step 4
Objective

What do I need an objective for?

I know what you are thinking – "My objective is to get a job that I want and STAT!" I agree. However, a clear and concise objective helps get your resume reviewed for the right position and conveys your career goals. Having a defined goal makes you look very good compared to someone who has a sketchy goal or no goal at all. You will want your objective to focus on the position or the employer or both. Keep in mind a few objectives to fit the appropriate position or employer. As stated before, you will want variations of your resume template to send to prospective employers. Never think in terms of one size fits all.

The objective is the first thing that the prospective employer will read so you want the objective to set the tone for the rest of your resume. If it is not in line with the employer's perspective, he/she may not view the rest of the resume. You should focus on three items of interest with a possible fourth item centering on your top skills. The objective should include the type of position (full time, part time, contract), the career field (marketing, accounting, engineering), the industry (medical, defense, environment), and the skills (organization, research, communication). Avoid being vague in your objective. You don't want an employer to think that you don't have a firm understanding of what you want and can do.

Your objective template should look something like this:

To secure a _____ position in _____ within a _____ with opportunity to use my strong _____ skills.

Here are some examples

OBJECTIVE: To secure a full-time management position in sales or promotions within a retail corporation with opportunity to use my strong organizational and communication skills.

OBJECTIVE: To secure an internship position to gain knowledge and experience in the field of publishing with a major consumer magazine.

OBJECTIVE: To secure a contract position with an engineering services agency to gain knowledge and experience in the military defense field.

OBJECTIVE: To secure a part-time high school teaching position within a city school district using my strong leadership skills.

OBJECTIVE: To secure an entry-level position as an accountant with a CPA firm in the pharmaceutical industry.

Easy – right?

Step 5
Experience

Note: Your worksheet will come in most handy here for building this section.

What is the significance of the Experience section?

This section shows your potential employer what you have accomplished to date. As the old saying goes - Other people judge us by what we have done, while we judge ourselves by what we can do. This is the section that you really need to think back and evaluate all of your past experiences especially the ones that pertain to your career goals.

Remember in Step 2 you were asked to complete a job search research? Did you do it? If you haven't, now is the time to complete it. This research will provide the guidance that you will need to organize your experiences to match the career you want. Plus you will know what language and style are appropriate for your dream position which should please your prospective employer.

The most important part of writing your experience is to show the employer the link to how your experience matches and relates to the job description. This is why it is important to study a few job descriptions in your chosen field. When writing your accomplishments and qualifications, remember to use the language you find within the position descriptions and the employers' websites. Keep in mind when listing your experiences to quantify and qualify as best as you can.

Right now, your goal is to write down every experience including volunteer work that will connect your experiences to the job you want. Get as many points down as you can. You will whittle it later for each resume your put together. You should save a master copy of your experience so you can pick and choose which will fit the appropriate job. In the future, as you gain more experience, you should add it to the list. This will make things easier when you need to update your resume for future endeavors.

The importance of language along with some examples is coming up in our next step.

Step 6
Language

Your resume should have effective language showing your experiences to the hiring official. You want to provide as best of a description as possible so the employer will believe you are a good fit for the company. There are many ways to build up your experience with words. In this step, you will learn how to use the employer's language, quantifying and qualifying, using parallel structure, and refraining from fluff.

Use the employer's language

Again, this is where your research will pay off. You will need to use the language of the employer and the industry. For example, if your chosen employer and industry value leadership traits, then you should consider titling your activities as "Leadership Experience." If the employer, industry or job description mentions strong management skills, then you should describe your past experiences and responsibilities using the word managed. If the position calls for training employees or clients, then make sure you describe your past experiences with the word trained. You get the picture? Using key words that match with the employer's terminology will get your resume noticed.

Use action verbs

When describing accomplishments, use strong action verbs. Here's a list of many strong action verbs that you can easily use to describe your accomplishments. This list is also available at http://www.integritycreativebusiness.com/resume-worksheet-templates.html (password is: 12easysteps).

abated	attacked	circulated	created
accelerated	attended	circumvented	credited
accomplished	audited	cited	critiqued
accounted for	augmented	clarified	cultivated
accumulated	authored	classified	decided
achieved	authorized	cleared	decreased
acquired	automated	closed	dedicated
acted	averted	coached	defended
activated	awarded	collaborated	defined
adapted	balanced	collected	deflected
added	began	combined	defrayed
addressed	benefited	comforted	defused
adjusted	bettered	commanded	delegated
administered	bid	commenced	delineated
advised	blocked	commissioned	delivered
adopted	blotted	committed	demonstrated
advanced	boosted	communicated	derived
advised	bought	compared	designated
advocated	bridled	compiled	designed
aided	briefed	completed	detailed
alerted	broadened	composed	determined
allayed	brokered	conceived	developed
alleviated	broke	conceptualized	devised
allocated	brought	concluded	devoted
allotted	budgeted	conducted	diminished
altered	built	conferred	directed
amassed	bundled	confirmed	discovered
amended	calculated	connected	dispatched
analyzed	calmed	conserved	displayed
annihilated	captured	consoled	disposed
answered	cared	consolidated	disrupted
anticipated	carried	constructed	disseminated
appeased	cataloged	consulted	dissolved
applied	catered	continued	distributed
appointed	caused	contracted	diversified
appraised	caught	contributed	divested
approached	celebrated	controlled	documented
appropriated	cemented	converted	doubled
approved	certified	conveyed	drafted
aroused	chaired	convinced	dramatized
arranged	challenged	cooperated	drove
ascended	changed	coordinated	earned
assembled	charged	corrected	eased
assessed	charted	corresponded	economized
assisted	checked	counseled	edited
assumed	chose	counted	educated
assured	chronicled	counteracted	elected

15

elicited	fought	invented	named
eliminated	founded	inventoried	narrowed
embraced	framed	interviewed	navigated
emphasized	fulfilled	invited	negotiated
employed	functioned	involved	negated
empowered	funded	isolated	netted
enabled	furthered	issued	networked
encouraged	gained	jacked up	neutralized
ended	garnered	joined	nominated
enforced	gathered	justified	notified
engaged	generated	kindled	nurtured
engineered	governed	knitted	observed
enhanced	graded	labored	obtained
enjoyed	graduated	launched	occupied
enlarged	greeted	learned	officiated
enlisted	grew	lectured	omitted
enriched	grossed	led	opened
enrolled	grouped	lengthened	operated
ensured	guided	lent	optimized
entered	handled	lessened	orchestrated
enticed	harnessed	leveled	ordered
equipped	headed	leveraged	organized
eradicated	healed	licensed	originated
established	heightened	lifted	outdistanced
estimated	held	limited	outlined
evaluated	helped	linked	outpaced
examined	highlighted	listened	out produced
exceeded	hoisted	located	overcame
excelled	hosted	made	overhauled
exchanged	housed	maintained	oversaw
executed	hunted	managed	paced
exercised	hurried	mandated	packaged
expanded	identified	maneuvered	packed
expedited	impacted	marked	paid
experienced	implemented	marketed	pared
experimented	imported	mastered	participated
explained	improved	maximized	partnered with
exposed	included	measured	penetrated
fabricated	incorporated	mediated	penned
facilitated	increased	mended	perceived
factored	ignited	mentored	performed
familiarized	incited	merged	persuaded
fashioned	influenced	merited	piloted
fielded	infused	met	pioneered
filed	initiated	minimized	placed
finalized	innovated	mobilized	planned
financed	inspected	moderated	played
finessed	inspired	modeled	practiced
focused	instilled	modified	praised
foresaw	instituted	molded	prepared
forged	instructed	monitored	presented
formed	integrated	motivated	preserved
formalized	interceded	mounted	prescribed
formulated	interpreted	moved	presided
forwarded	intervened	multiplied	prevented
fostered	introduced	nailed	printed

prioritized
processed
procured
produced
profiled
profited
programmed
progressed
projected
progressed
promoted
proposed
proved
provided
pruned
publicized
published
purchased
pursued
pushed
qualified
quantified
quelled
quickened
quieted
quoted
raced
ratcheted
raided
raised
rallied
ran
ranked
rated
reached
realized
rebuilt
received
recognized
recommended
reconciled
reconstructed
recorded
recovered
recruited
rectified
redirected
reduced
reengineered
registered
regulated
reinforced
reinvigorated
released

relieved
remained
remodeled
renegotiated
renewed
reorganized
repaired
replaced
reported
represented
researched
resolved
restored
restricted
restructured
retained
retooled
retrieved
returned
revamped
revealed
reversed
reviewed
revised
revitalized
revived
revolutionized
rewarded
safeguarded
salvaged
saved
saw
scheduled
screened
scrutinized
searched
secured
seized
selected
sensitized
sent
sequenced
served
set
settled
shaped
sharpened
shrank
shortened
showed
sifted
simplified
simulated
smoothed

snagged
sold
solicited
solved
sought
sourced
spearheaded
specialized
specified
speeded
split
spoke
sponsored
spurred
stabilized
started
stated
steered
stimulated
stopped
strategized
streamlined
strengthened
stretched
stripped
studied
submitted
succeeded
suggested
summarized
supervised
supplied
supported
surpassed
surveyed
synthesized
systemized
tackled
tagged
taught
tended
terminated
tested
theorized
thrived
tied
topped
took
took over
tooled
totaled
toughened
toured
towered

traced
tracked
trained
transacted
transcended
transferred
transformed
translated
transmitted
transported
traveled
trebled
triggered
trimmed
tripled
troubleshot
turned around
tutored
uncovered
undertook
unified
united
upgraded
upheld
upstaged
used
utilized
validated
valued
vaulted
verified
vitalized
vocalized
voiced
volleyed
volunteered
voted
waded
weakened
weathered
whipped
widened
withstood
won over
worked
wove
wrote
yielded

Quantify and qualify

When showing your related experiences and responsibilities, you will need to do more than restate the job description. You can accomplish this by quantifying and qualifying whenever you can. For example:

- If you worked as a budget analyst, you should put in the size of the budget that you analyzed
- If you trained employees at a past job, then include the number of employees in total with whom you have trained
- If you worked as a graphic designer, you should list the software used to put together for your campaigns
- If you taught elementary school students, then you should note the age of the students and how many students in each level of proficiency

Examples

From this:
Responsible for supervising employees

To this:
Supervised 12 salespeople, 5 cashiers and 2 service desk representatives

From this:
Worked on setting up a SharePoint page

To this:
Designed and developed a SharePoint site involving 55 pages using Dreamweaver software

From this:
Responsible for all aspects of annual wine festival fundraiser

To this:
Coordinated with 25 vendors, designed marketing and promotional materials including print and TV ads, flyers, and programs; organized and scheduled 75 volunteers; and managed a $100,000 budget for the annual Colorado Springs wine festival fundraiser

Use parallel language

When writing your experiences, you need to be consistent and use parallel language. Parallel language is using the same structure for each entry. Typically, entries are written starting with strong action verbs to describe the experience. Make sure the verb tense is the same. You should use past-tense verbs with past experiences and present-tense verbs with present responsibilities.

Here is an example that doesn't use parallel language:

XYZ Company – Denver, CO   January 8, 2010 – March 19, 2012
Event Planner

- Was responsible for coordinating 18 vendors
- Print ads, brochures, flyers, and programs
- organize 75 volunteers
- Managed a $90,000 budget for the annual fundraiser wine festival

Here is an example that does use parallel language:

XYZ Company – Denver, CO   January 8, 2010 – March 19, 2012
Event Planner

- Coordinated arrangements with 18 vendors
- Designed marketing materials including print ads, brochures, flyers, and programs
- Organized the schedule for 75 volunteers
- Managed a $90,000 budget for the annual fundraiser wine festival

Avoid fluff

You will do well if you refrain from using material that does not apply to the prospective job. You only need to include information that the employers will want to know so that they can make a determination if you are the person they want to hire. The employer doesn't care if you won the New York City marathon unless you are applying for a physical trainer type of position.

Remember:

- Include everything that is important to marketing yourself for the job.
- Keep out everything else
- Use clear and concise language. You don't need flowery adjectives and useless adverbs. In other words, Get to the point!

Step 7
Education

The education section is a significant element to include in your resume.

What information should I put in the Education section?

If you have a degree or certificate from an accredited school, you should certainly put it on your resume. You should list each degree and certificate starting with the latest in descending order. Start with the institution and its location where you received your degree/certificate. The degree information – such as Bachelor of Sciences in Business Management - should go on the next line along with the date your received your degree. Your GPA (grade point average) will go on the third line; you may include both your major GPA and your cumulative GPA. (You may want to skip the GPA line if your GPA falls below a 3.0.) Add in any honors or points of interest (e.g., studying abroad) on the next line if you feel this is beneficial for the position that you are applying for. Usually it is! On that note, you may want to add on the final line any related or relevant coursework to the position that you are applying for especially if the position is outside of the realm of your degree. Do this for each degree that you have. Don't worry about putting college information pertaining to coursework you did before you transferred to a different school. Use only the schools where you got the official degree.

Where does the Education section go?

Immediately after the objective for:

- Current undergraduate students pursuing a summer job, internship, fellowship, or co-op position
- Graduates who are pursuing their first professional position
- Advanced degree graduates who need the credentials for their advancement in the career that they are pursuing

After the experience section when:

- Seeking advancement within the career field and it has been a few years since the degree was completed

- Using the functional resume style which involves listing experiences within skill areas related to the sought-after career, followed by the degree field which is not closely related to the career being pursued
- Having already acquired substantial professional experience in the field - even if the advanced degree is also related to the field. Professional experience will carry more weight while the advanced degree will support the advancement

What else should you include in the Education section?

Don't sweat it if you do not have a college degree or certificate. You may add any college courses you have taken even if it didn't lead to a degree or certificate. If you don't have any college experience at all, put in your high school information – where you went to high school, date graduated, and of course, put in any classes you took that may apply to the job you are applying for. For example, I took several business classes during my high school years. Before I had my college degree, I put my high school information in the education section along with a list of the classes I took – accounting, business management, etc. However, I would not include your high school information if you already have a college degree.

Reflect on the training that you have acquired during your work life that can be included in this section. Most jobs provide some kind of training that you can include here. Also, don't forget to include adult education classes, YMCA classes, military training, specialty schools such as vocational training, and any other classes you may have taken to advance yourself whether it is for a hobby or work. Please include only relevant classes to the job you are applying for. Remember you can tailor each resume to the prospective job. Don't forget to include any certifications in this section such as real estate licenses. Label this training as Professional Development. If you have specific training for the prospective job, you may want to put it in its own section. For instance, in the below example, there is a special section devoted to writing training. This is what I put in my writer's resume. Every time you take a class, get a certificate or a new degree, add it to the resume. I bet you didn't realize how much education you really have!

Here is an example to use as a template

The Pennsylvania State University – University Park, PA
Bachelor of Arts in Letters, Arts and Science   December 2011
    Major GPA: 3.96   Cumulative GPA: 3.83
        Dean's List, The Honor Society of Phi Kappa Phi, Penn State Pi Delta Chi Chapter of Alpha
        Sigma Lambda, National Society of Collegiate Scholars

Associate of Arts in Letters, Arts and Science   December 2008
   GPA: 4.0
      Dean's List

Certificate in Writing for Social Commentary   December 2008
      Relevant Courses: Critical Thinking, Rhetoric and Composition, Effective Writing:
                     Writing in Social Sciences, Article Writing, Magazine Writing,
                     Creative Writing

Professional Development:
Theater of Arts, Los Angeles, CA, Major: Theater, Movie, TV Production
Jan Nagy Modeling and Finishing School, Allentown, PA (Etiquette, Public Speaking,
Protocol)

Writing Training:
Effective Writing Skills, Foundations of Grammar, Communication/Interpersonal Skills
Training, High-Impact Business Writing Workshop, Presentation Skills

Step 8
Activities

For most jobs, you will want to show your leadership and community involvement whether that be in a professional organization or community association. You can title it "Leadership Experience" or simply "Activities." To show leadership skills, you should demonstrate how you have gone above and beyond normal expectations, took the initiative, and facilitated a team or group. You should also include what position you held within those organizations.

What should you put in the Activities section?

- The name of the organization
- The position held
- What you accomplished in that position
- Keep your experiences to about 3 – 5 positions

Should you include political activities?

It's not uncommon for someone to belong to an organization or association that has political connotations. There is nothing wrong with being affiliated with most of these organizations, but your resume is not the place where you want to advertise it. This is in no way stating that you shouldn't be who you are!

The exception would be if you are looking for a position within the organization or the company that you want to work for supports your political cause.

Always list your activities in the order of importance to you. Why? Because this is how the prospective employer will view it as well.

Where should you list any honors or distinctions you received in school?

If you are or were some whiz kid or decorated soldier, you could put your activities and honors together in one section. Perhaps it can be titled "Activities and Honors" or "Honors and Activities" which section is titled first should be what you start with. Once again, the ones that are most important to you should go first. You can also separate the two if you have numerous entries that you want to list. Also, honors and distinctions may be listed in the Education section under the school and degree for which the honors were received. If you have a military background, you should put them where you put your military experience.

EXAMPLES:

HONORS & ACTIVITIES

NSF Graduate Research Fellowship Recipient

Committee on Women in Science, Engineering and Medicine, Chairperson

Junior Achievement, Volunteer

ACTIVITIES

National Society of Accountants
Professional Development Committee

Intramural Sports
basketball, tennis, volleyball

ACTIVITIES

President – Women's History Month
Led weekly meetings and organized various events during the month

Secretary – March of Dimes, Utah Chapter
Organized participation and scheduled volunteers for March of Dimes walkathons

Marketing Committee – La Bella Dance Troupe

Step 9
Skills

You may have skills that don't necessarily fit in the other sections of your resume. However, you still want to include them. You can create a Skills section in your resume. Skills can range from computer knowledge that you may have to foreign languages that you speak. If you want to stand out from the rest of them, you should consider what other skills you have that you want to include in your resume.

What type of categories can you put in the Skills section?

Here are some suggestions:

Computer Skills – List software, hardware, and coding that you are familiar with

Foreign Languages – Indicate your level of proficiency such as elementary, conversational, fluent or native. You should also list whether that is reading, writing or speaking or a combination of all three

Travel – If you have extensive travel experience, write a brief synopsis of no more than 3 – 5 lines about it

See the examples at the end of the chapter for reference.

Should you list all of your skills?

You should refrain from putting in skills that are not conducive to the job that you are applying for. These skills should tie in with your objective and job description. Be careful on what you include because as much as you want the prospective employers to think that you are interesting and perfect for the job, you also don't want them to wonder why you are putting unrelated information on your resume. You don't want the prospective employers to think that you do not understand what the position and company are all about.

Where should you put the Skills section?

Regardless of the type of resume you choose to use, the Skills sections should be listed after the Experience section of your resume.

Here are some examples:

SKILLS

> Extensive knowledge of Microsoft Word, Excel, Access, PowerPoint, Lotus Notes, Website Development

> Proficient in Japanese

COMPUTER SKILLS

> Developed procedures for IBM environments

> Resolved security and capacity issues using TMON/DB2, TMON/MVS, SDSF, RMF monitor, Cloning Tool, Buffer Pool Analyzer

> Maintained Database Management systems

Step 10
References

You may simply state "References Available Upon Request" centered at the end of your resume. What you should do is develop a separate 'References' page that you can print out and take with you to interviews. Sometimes references are requested in the application and you can just attach your References page to your resume or as a separate attachment. Usually there will be instructions within the application that will tell you how the company wants your references should it be a requirement.

Who should you put on your References page? You need to think about the people who will give great recommendations about you that will show you are qualified for the position. These people can be former employers, advisors, faculty members, mentors and teachers. Personal references are not typically the best people to include unless they have connections with the organization that will benefit you getting the job.

How should you format your References page?

- Obviously you should title it References in bold and center it on the top of the page
- Put your full name underneath the title
- Your reference's information such as job title, business name, business address, business phone number and business email
- Your relationship with the person such as former supervisor, mentor or professor
- You should list your references in alphabetical order by last name
- You should have at least two but no more than six references. Most people use three references

Here's how your References page should look:

REFERENCES

Jane A.
Doe

Ms. Mary B. Jones
Director of Human Resources
XYZ Company
938 Long Street
San Diego, CA 92019
619-888-7777
maryjones@xyzco.com
(former director at XYZ Company)

Mr. John Smith
Program Manager
ABC Corporation
555 Main Street
San Diego, CA 92019
619-111-2222
jsmith@abccorp.com
(former supervisor at ABC Corporation)

Dr. Susan D. Yates
Professor of Symbolic Logic
San Diego State University
202 Campus Drive
San Diego, CA 92019
619-333-4444
sdy@sdsu.edu
(former professor at San Diego State University)

Step 11
Formatting

In this step, you will learn how to format your resume for a professional look.

How long should your resume be?

Despite what you may have been told, you do not need to keep your resume to one page unless the submissions guidelines state otherwise. However, you may lose their interest after the first few pages. A good rule of thumb is to have no more than three pages and make sure the pages are full with minimal white space. You can always adjust the font and margins to fit the resume into three pages so long as you don't make the font size so small that your prospective employer needs a magnifying glass to read it.

What is the basic page setup for each resume?

- Margins should be set to 0.5" up to 1.0" top, bottom, left and right
- Times New Roman or Arial font with either a 10 or 12 point pitch are your best choices. Avoid fancy fonts. They can be difficult to read especially since employers use different computer platforms
- Stick with black for your font color no matter how creative the job may be
- Headings can be bolded or underscored for emphasis but do not put the whole resume in bold. Also avoid highlighting text in various colors or any color for that matter
- Bullets are great for listing your credentials and experience.
- Templates from word processing programs are fine for style but remember that the content is the most important part of the resume. What's in the resume is what will get you hired
- Don't be clever by changing the background color to anything but white or changing the orientation to landscape. Show your creativity in your words or your portfolio – not in your formatting!
- Save your resume using this naming convention "Your Name Resume." For example, my resume name is Connie Schlosberg Resume (connieschlosbergresume.doc).

Step 12
Distribution

In this step, you will:

- Learn how to use keywords to increase your chances of being selected as a candidate for the job
- Learn how to save your resume in different types of file formats

Keywords

Like it or not, keywords are used to find resumes uploaded to employer jobsites and online job boards. Keywords provide the information from which to search for a resume in a database that connects job searchers with employers for specific jobs.

Keywords describe your knowledge and experiences and make the connection from you to the position you are pursuing. Your job search research should have identified possible words that will connect your skills and accomplishments to the job you want. The best keywords are nouns such as "Manager" in place of "managed" or "managing" or terms that are specific to the field such as "Systems Analysis" in place of "analyzed systems".

What makes a good keyword?

- Nouns and phrases that highlight technical and professional areas of expertise
- Industry-related terminology
- Project titles
- Achievements
- Special task force or committee work
- Other distinctive features about your work history related to the position you are pursuing

You should wait until you have finished writing your resume before you insert your keywords section. Think of all the words an employer would use to search for your position or skills. Place your keyword section after your objective or as the final section of your resume. You may integrate the keywords you have identified into the text of your resume similar to how websites use SEO (Search Engine Optimization).

Keyword Summary Example for a Systems Analyst

Systems Analysis. Systems Integration. Network Administration. Database Administration. Systems Administration. Troubleshooting Computing Systems. C++. Visual Basic. SQL. UNIX Shell Script. Windows. MS DOS. Windows XP. TCP/IP. OSI. Microsoft LAN Manager. Novell Netware. Project Management. Trade Studies. Consulting. BETA Tester. Technical Presentations. Sales Presentations. Instructor. BS Degree. Mathematics and Computer Science.

Distribution

Many employers are adamant about accepting resumes in certain formats only. Some employers will ask you to copy and paste your resume within the body of an email. You should save your resume in different formats so that you will have them ready when you need to send it rather than having to put it together at the last minute. You should send your resume to yourself both as an attachment and in the body of the email so you can view the final version that the employer would receive. In this way, you will know if the resume is formatted correctly and is readable rather than scrambled which may cause an employer to simply delete your email. (You don't want that to happen!)

You should have one version of your resume that is stripped of special formatting that may not translate for applications that require you to cut and paste your resume. Some job board sites will advise you if you need to remove special formatting from your resume. Specials formats that you will need to change or remove are:

> **Bullets** – Change bullets to either asterisks (*) or hyphens (-) at the beginning of each line

> **Numbering** – Change automatic numbering to either asterisks (*) or hyphens (-) at the beginning of each line

> **Lines** – Change lines to a series of dashes to separate sections (--------------------)

> **Bold Text** - Change bold text to ALLCAPS instead

> **Italicized Text** – Change italicized text to plain text

> **Underlined Text** – Change underlined text to plain text

> **Highlighted Text** – You shouldn't have any highlighted text; nonetheless, you will need to remove it

Another format you may want to consider is saving your resume in Rich Text Format using the extension ".rtf." This format is accepted because of its compatibility across word processing software. Usually the employer or the job board site will indicate if you need to save your resume in Rich Text Format. You may as well keep a version of your resume already saved as rtf so it's one less thing to do when applying for jobs. To save your resume as Rich Text Format, simply select "Save As" and select Rich Text Format as your file type from the drop-down list selections (e.g., janedoeresume.rtf).

You're all set! Let's take a look at other ways to sell yourself. Yep, you read that right. Go sell yourself.

Bonus Step
Personal Branding

Now you have your resume written and ready to send to your prospective employers. Resumes are still the traditional way to get hired for most positions whether it is full-time, part-time, contract, internship and even freelance. However, in the 21st century you need to know how to market yourself.

Marketing and promotions isn't just for organizations anymore my friends.

If you are anything like me, you may despise the thought of selling yourself to anyone or any organization. The thought of shaking hands and a saying "How do you do" draws smarmy pictures of cigar smoking greasy handed old men in my head. Yours, too? No worries. There are other ways of promoting yourself without the cold calls and networking parties.

Social Media. There are as many social media sites as there are people or so it seems. The big ones are LinkedIn and Facebook with Google+, Pinterest and Tumblr coming up and running. They are easy to setup. If you can read, you can setup a social media site.

LinkedIn is the site for business relations and networking. You can join and participate in groups in your area of interests and follow and research companies that you may want to work for. Each company shows a list of people who work there with LinkedIn accounts. You can ask for introductions from people who are your connections with their connections who may be able to help you in your job search.

You can also be bold and send a message directly to the connection. Be polite and let the person know who you are and what you are looking for. Get to the point and keep it short. If you don't hear back from him/her, move on. Don't waste time on someone who has no interest in helping you. However, keep in mind that you should not just ask for help. Show them how you can benefit the company by focusing on how you are going to help them. You must make them subliminally think that you are looking to help them rather than the other way around.

When you post on your social media site, share something that is useful for those in your field such as an interesting article, commenting on relevant industry news, sharing accomplishments and joining online debates.

In LinkedIn, Look for your peers at companies in your industry and review their profiles to see what is similar and what is different. Also, look at the Companies' pages in LindedIn to gain insight on the people the company has hired and even those who have left to see what type of positions they are looking for. Then look at their growth to see if they are growing, shrinking or just flat.

Blogs. You can start a blog in minutes and for free. Don't think that blogs are just for writers and soccer moms or soccer mom writers. Blogs are a great way to showcase who you are and what you can do or what you are an expert in. Believe me – there is something you can blog about no matter what type of work you do.

Here are a few quick ways to figure out what you can write about:

- What do your family, friends, co-workers, etc. ask you for help with? Can you translate that information into regular posts on your blog?
- What are you passionate about that you can correlate your blog to what you want to do for a living?
- What do you like to share with others that you are knowledgeable about? Maybe that knowledge can be offered via a blog.

Of course, just like social media sites, there are lots of sites that offer free blogs such as **www.blogger.com** and **www.wordpress.com** that are easy to setup and start posting.

YouTube. Are you good at making videos? I applied for two jobs online that asked if I had any videos to show them what I can do. The only video that I had created was a cooking segment of my family and me demonstrating how to make chili bean soup. I wasn't sure if this was apropos for the job so I hesitated about sending it. Now I regret it because it showed my personality and the job called for a PR person.

Even if you are not in the video business, you may want to consider creating videos that represent what you can do such as an instructional video and upload them for free to YouTube. If you have enough videos, you can create a video channel on YouTube. Videos aren't just for creative types, but if you appear awkward on camera you may want to skip this form of personal branding. For the rest of you, film away. You never know. You may become a YouTube sensation.

Websites. Depending on your budget, you may want to consider setting up a website. A website can be viewed as a form of advertisement for you. Websites entail time and money to operate. If you are not savvy with technology, you may have to hire someone to do it for you. This can get expensive. I once hired outside help to create a website for a company that I used to own. It cost me over $2,000 for a basic design, and I had to write the content for the website. If you don't write, you will have to hire someone to write it for you.

Nonetheless, if you are a professional, creative type or a freelancer, a website is the perfect venue for showcasing who you are and how to get in touch with you. If you have it search engine optimized (another cost if you are not a tech expert), then people will find you easy through web searches without having to pay for advertisements on the internet.

Not all websites are expensive if you can get away with a simple website. Most people can get away with a basic one page website. You can use the user-friendly Weebly (www.weebly.com) to design your basic website for free. You will build it yourself through a series of setups that the system walks you through. You just have to pay for the domain name which you can get for less than $20 per year via GoDaddy (www.godaddy.com). (There are plenty of sites that offer cheap domains; simply search for "cheap domains" and you bound to find to suit you.)

Online Portfolios. Creative types will definitely need an online portfolio to show off their great creations. However, I wouldn't brush off having a portfolio if you are in a different field. Are there some documents such as policies, procedures, internal communications that you created for work, school or charity? I bet if you search around and truly think about it, you will come up with some items. Did you create a spreadsheet or financial tracker that absolutely stunned everyone in the accounting department or even just amused them? How about an article that you wrote for the company newsletter? Think hard. Be creative. Use your lateral thinking – Problem solving through unconventional and illogical means.

Online portfolios can have fees attached to them so you may want to start with free ones if your budget is tight. Crevado offers free online portfolios at www.crevado.com.

Magazines and Newspaper Advertisements. This is a potentially high-cost measure for promoting yourself, but it can be successful particularly if you are pursuing freelance and contract work. Even so, you may want to give it a try if you are looking to market you talents for a new position.

Which magazines and newspapers? I would look at ones that pertain to your field such as trade magazines. Local newspapers are great if you want to market yourself within your community. Consumer magazines may be trickier unless you have a product or service that is tailored to consumers rather than businesses. If you don't know if there is a trade magazine for your field, simply search on "[your trade]" and "magazine and newspapers and publications," I'm sure something is bound to come up. You would be surprised at how many publications exist. Not all of them are sold in bookstores, which, unfortunately, are becoming extinct anyway.

Think outside the box: alumni magazines and newsletters, church/synagogue bulletins, Craig's List (www.craigslist.com). What else? Anytime you see advertisements in publications think if it will be a good place for you to advertise as well.

The Old Standbys – Networking and Cold Calling. For those of you who are brave social butterflies, both networking and cold calling can do wonders for getting your name out there and landing the jobs that you want. The rest of us need to learn how to be social butterflies to reap the same benefits.

Spread the message by letting friends, co-workers, family members and former supervisors know that you are looking for work. You can try and introduce yourself to hiring managers at the organizations where you want to work and learn more about the position you are interested in. (Don't ask for a job or referral; you're just there to gather information.)

You can create your own business cards using your computer's software programs or you can have them printed professionally. Try to attend career events and industry seminars to interact with others in your field. You can even try to set up informational meetings with executives and managers to chat about your career. Just think where it may lead.

What else? Always remember that there are many ways that you can market yourself. Years ago there was a model/actress names Angelyne who paid for billboard advertisements of herself which were placed around Hollywood and Los Angeles. It worked. She essentially became notorious, leading to parts in movies and television.

You never know. You just have to be clever.

Remember if you do have a blog, YouTube channel, website, and/or online portfolio, make sure you put the link in your resume preferably in the header section.

One caveat about personal branding: Don't put anything out there about yourself that you wouldn't want you mother to see (or any mother to see for that matter.)

Closing Thoughts

By now you should have a stellar resume or set of resumes uploaded to job sites and even submitted to prospective jobs. I hope you found the process fairly easy and have great success in using your resume to get the job that you truly want. I know what it feels like to be overwhelmed by something such as writing a resume when you don't know how to approach it.

That is why I started this 12 Easy Steps program. For people who simply want to learn how to do something and have a final product by the end of the program. I've read, written, and edited enough how-to and instructional products to know that sometimes there is too much information given, which can slow a person down, who is simply trying to learn and have something to show for it. Remember what I said about paralysis by analysis? You don't want to go there.

That said, if you get stuck while comprising your resume during the course of this e-book, please feel free to email me one question at info@integritycreativebusiness.com. I will reply back with an answer within three business days.

Please keep in mind that you are important and even though looking for those perfect gigs can be challenging –job hunting is a job within itself – you will find what you are looking for if you keep at it. Keep in mind that you should spend your time on the creative plane rather than the competitive one. If you only think a limited amount of jobs are out there, then only a limited amount of people can fill them. That is not true. You can create work. You just need to put the effort in. There is something that you can do and get paid for.

One last thing: Never, ever, ever, ever give up! Don't let the naysayers win.

Why the *12 Easy Steps* workbook program?

I know you are busy. You have a lot on your plate and sometimes you just want to cut to the chase on how to get something done. I've held a lot of hands in my time and I want to hold yours, too. My e-books are available all on your devices. You'll have me right there in your home, office, or favorite spot on the beach (my favorite too!).

I just want you to be able to learn to do something as quick and easy as possible without the long wait. I know. You want a final product after you read how to do something. You want humor. You want thoughtfulness. You want insight. But you don't want fluff. Or technical jargon. .And you want to do it in a *quick-read-it-and-get-it done* way.

I've read enough how-to, instructional, and informational books, and all of them were wonderful. Okay. Perhaps not all of them. They gave me ways to percolate and think about the subject, but not all them gave me a quick and easy, get down and dirty, *here let's do it now together or get off your ass and get it done* concrete workbook. After all, you want to get it done – right?

When using these workbooks, you work on your creation as you read so that when you finish the workbook, you have your finished product.

About Me

I was bitten by the writing bug ever since I started writing poetry in the sixth grade. Many moons later, I still enjoy writing. I received my Bachelor's Degree in Letters, Arts and Sciences and have a *Writing for Social Commentary* certificate with the Pennsylvania State University. I attended the Theatre of Arts in Los Angeles and have appeared in the Disney movie, My Secret Bodyguard. Published poetry includes "Lock and Key" featured in *A Far Off Place* and "Roses Will Bloom" in *Stories of Strength* and most recently, a chapbook *1340,* aptly named for the time between when the poems were written.

I am a freelance writer with credits from a variety of publications, recently including The Colorado Springs Gazette, The Space Observer, and Mom Writers Literary Magazine. I have written and edited for numerous organizations such as Century 21, Polymer Corporation, and of course, the ever exciting Department of Defense. I've spent many years writing resumes for business professionals, consulting with human resources specialists and senior level managers on what they are looking at when reviewing resumes.

When surfing the net, stop by www.connieschlosberg.com. I don't just write for pleasure; I write for business as well. Please visit www.integritycreativebusiness.com for more information.

My Job Line

This should explain everything.

Babysitter	6 years
Bookkeeper	6 months
Customer Service Representative	2 months
Marketing and PR	1 year and 11 months
Office Manager	20 years
Sales Clerk	1 year and 10 months
UNEMPLOYED	2 years and 2 months
Waitress	2 days
Writer/Artist/All-Around-Pain-in-the-Ass	45 years

Well – what are you waiting for? Is that resume written? Did you upload it to every job board in your field (oh hell - even outside your field)?

Go do it!

Worksheets

NAME_____

Address_____

City, State ZIP Code_____

Home Phone No._____

Work Phone No._____

Cell Phone No._____

Email Address_____

OBJECTIVE

To secure a _____ position in _____ within the _____ with opportunity to use my strong _____ skills.

EMPLOYMENT HISTORY

> List up to 10 years of work if possible. You don't need to reflect back past 10 years unless those jobs are related to the job you're applying for now. List in chronological order starting with the latest position.

Position Title_____

First Employer Name, City, ST_____

Dates Employed_____

Experience_____

_____

_____

_____

_____

_____

Position Title_____

Second Employer Name, City, ST_____

Dates Employed_____

Experience_____

_____

_____

_____

_____

_____

Position Title_____

Third Employer Name, City, ST_____

Dates Employed_____

Experience_____

_____

_____

_____

_____

_____

Position Title_____

Fourth Employer Name, City, ST_____

Dates Employed_____

Experience_____

_____

_____

_____

_____

_____

Be sure to include Name and Location of School, Degree including Graduation Month and Year, Your Major and Possibly Your GPA. You can include your coursework and honors information here as well.

EDUCATION

_____

_____

_____

_____

_____

_____

_____

_____

_____

_____

_____

SPECIAL SKILLS

_____

_____

_____

_____

_____

ACTIVITIES

_____

_____

_____

_____

_____

NOTES

_____

_____

_____

_____

_____

_____

_____

NAME_____

Address_____

City, State ZIP Code_____

Home Phone No._____

Work Phone No._____

Cell Phone No._____

Email Address_____

OBJECTIVE

To secure a _____ position in _____ within the _____ with opportunity to use my strong _____ skills.

RELATED SKILLS

_____(First Skill Area)

- _____
- _____
- _____
- _____
- _____
- _____
- _____

_____(Second Skill Area)

- _____
- _____
- _____
- _____
- _____
- _____
- _____

_____(Third Skill Area)

- _____
- _____
- _____
- _____
- _____
- _____
- _____

_____(Fourth Skill Area)

- _____
- _____
- _____
- _____
- _____
- _____

> Be sure to include Name and Location of School, Degree including Graduation Month and Year, Your Major and Possibly Your GPA. You can include your coursework and honors information here as well.

EDUCATION

_____

_____

_____

_____

_____

_____

_____

_____

_____

_____

_____

EMPLOYMENT HISTORY

First Employer Name – City, ST   *Position Title*   (dates)

Second Employer Name – City, ST   *Position Title*   (dates)

Third Employer Name – City, ST   *Position Title*   (dates)

Fourth Employer Name – City, ST   *Position Title*   (dates)

_____

_____

_____

_____

_____

_____

SPECIAL SKILLS

_____

_____

_____

_____

_____

_____

ACTIVITIES

_____

_____

_____

_____

_____

_____

NOTES

NAME_____

Address_____

City, State ZIP Code_____

Home Phone No._____

Work Phone No._____

Cell Phone No._____

Email Address_____

OBJECTIVE

To secure a _____ position in _____ within the _____ with opportunity to use my strong _____ skills.

RELATED SKILLS

_____(First Skill Area)

- _____
- _____
- _____
- _____
- _____
- _____
- _____

_____(Second Skill Area)

- _____
- _____
- _____
- _____
- _____
- _____
- _____

_____(Third Skill Area)

- _____
- _____
- _____
- _____
- _____
- _____
- _____

_____(Fourth Skill Area)

- _____
- _____
- _____
- _____
- _____

EMPLOYMENT HISTORY

> List up to 10 years of work if possible. You don't need to reflect back past 10 years unless those jobs are related to the job you're applying for now. List in chronological order starting with the latest position.

Position Title_____

First Employer Name, City, ST_____

Dates Employed_____

Experience_____

_____

_____

_____

_____

_____

Position Title_____

Second Employer Name, City, ST_____

Dates Employed_____

Experience_____

_____

_____

_____

_____

_____

Position Title_____

Third Employer Name, City, ST_____

Dates Employed_____

Experience_____

_____

_____

_____

_____

Position Title_____

Fourth Employer Name, City, ST_____

Dates Employed_____

- Experience_____

_____

_____

_____

_____

_____

_____

Be sure to include Name and Location of School, Degree including Graduation Month and Year, Your Major and Possibly Your GPA. You can include your coursework and honors information here as well.

EDUCATION

_____

_____

_____

_____

_____

_____

_____

_____

_____

_____

_____

_____

SPECIAL SKILLS

_____

_____

_____

_____

_____

_____

ACTIVITIES

_____

_____

_____

_____

_____

_____

NOTES